Bygone Glasgow

Martin Jenkins and Ian Stewart

Ian Allan
PUBLISHING

This book is dedicated to Barry 'Curly' Cross, without whose generosity and support for both the Scottish Tramway and Transport Society and Online Transport Archive this all-colour album would not have been possible.

Front cover: Sauchiehall Street, probably the best known of all Glasgow's streets, is primarily residential at its west end but east of Charing Cross is a mix of shops, hotels, commercial premises and places of entertainment. This photograph was taken on 3 June 1960. The following day trams ceased serving this section.
E. C. Bennett and Martin Jenkins / Online Transport Archive

Back cover: Generations of Glaswegians loved standing on George V Bridge to watch *Queen Mary II* depart on her 11am 'doon the watter' sailing from Bridge Wharf. To be on board provided an exciting escape from the grime and grind of city life. Sadly, loadings declined and the cruises ended in 1969. *Marcus Eavis / Online Transport Archive*

Previous page: Until the mid-1950s Glasgow was a great tramway city, although many older cars were in need of replacement. Glasgow Bridge (also known as Jamaica Bridge) was rebuilt in 1899 from an earlier Thomas Telford structure. This view, dating from May 1955 and showing the line of centre poles, provides an idea of the intensity of service. *Ray DeGroote / Online Transport Archive*

Right: This aerial view clearly shows the gridiron pattern of streets in the central business district. The tiny green area is Blythswood Square. The need to negotiate many right-angled turns had dictated the length and profile of the Corporation-built trams.
Ian Stewart collection

First published 2010

ISBN 978 0 7110 3430 3

Published by Ian Allan Publishing

an imprint of Ian Allan Publishing Ltd, Hersham, Surrey, KT12 4RG

Printed in England by Ian Allan Printing Ltd, Hersham, Surrey, KT12 4RG

Code: 1006/B

Distributed in the United States of America and Canada by BookMasters Distribution services

Visit the Ian Allan Publishing website at www.ianallanpublishing.com

Introduction

How to define 'Bygone Glasgow'? Each generation will retain memories of *their* Glasgow, but, to survive, all cities have to change and evolve, and for each generation some of those changes are for the better, and some for the worse. Glasgow has been no exception. The earliest colour image in this book dates from 1949, when the city was in the grip of postwar austerity and few people could have envisaged the profound changes which lay ahead. Evidence of war damage remained, especially in the Burgh of Clydebank, which had been heavily bombed. Many were hoping for improvements to their standard of living, particularly better housing, and some would have known of plans to relocate people in vast housing estates. On the transport front, lengthy queues were matched by intensive, high-frequency services, and few people gave much thought to their immediate environs as they waited in all kinds of weather, anxious to get from A to B as quickly as possible. It mattered little if they travelled by steam train, chain ferry, tram, bus or the recently introduced trolleybuses.

As late as the mid-1950s few Glaswegians could have predicted that in the not too distant future *their* port, together with its shipping, would all but disappear, and the world-renowned shipbuilding output be severely reduced; that trips 'doon the watter' would cease together, as would all but one of the cross-river ferries; that much labour-intensive heavy industry would evaporate; that cinemas, theatres and churches would close; that thriving shopping areas would decline as out-of-town complexes were opened and shopping and travel patterns were revised accordingly; that busy intersections such as Anderston Cross, Charing Cross, St George's Cross and Govan Cross would be swept away and all manner of buildings torn down, often without due care and thought; that some of the city's most famous streets would be partially pedestrianised; that the familiar trams would disappear and the new-fangled trolleybuses have a short shelf-life;

Full skirts are in fashion as crowds flock to the Kelvin Hall in 1959, then the city's principal events venue. This time it was the Scottish Industries Exhibition — when Scotland still had industries to exhibit! The 'Coronation' tram (left), eastbound with a full load, has just crossed Partick Bridge, whilst in the background are the adjoining campuses of the Western Infirmary and Glasgow University. Destined to be replaced in 1985 by the Scottish Exhibition & Conference Centre (SECC), the Kelvin Hall incorporated the Museum of Transport from 1988 until 2010.
Ian Stewart

that conductors would be phased out; that buses would emerge without rear platforms; that houses would cease to use coal for heating; that diesel and electric trains would oust steam and rationalisation of the railways lead to the closure of lines and stations; that a dramatic rise in car ownership would create demand for improved vehicle access to the city as well as increased car parking; that fashions would alter, street furniture would be removed and the last horse-drawn carts, already redolent of another 'bygone' age, would clip-clop into history.

For centuries Glasgow was a small but important academic and theological centre, home to a university and cathedral, although few buildings survive from this early period. Glasgow was transformed by the union with England, the

Inbound company buses were not permitted to pick up passengers within the Glasgow city boundary nor drop them off on outbound journeys. This protection for Corporation services did not apply outside the city limits, where there were no such inhibitions. The rivalry was particularly intense between Paisley and Renfrew Ferry. Thus, when the highly profitable trams were abandoned in 1957, it was independent operators like Paton's of Renfrew that grabbed the passengers. This all-Leyland TD7 of 1942 had been acquired by Paton's from Glasgow Corporation in 1958 and was one of a number of buses on which construction had begun during the early days of World War 2 only to be stopped and then 'unfrozen'. *Marcus Eavis / Online Transport Archive*

Besides being a world centre for locomotive building Glasgow had major locomotive works and a number of motive-power depots. Until 1964 Polmadie shed had housed and serviced the ex-LMS Stanier Pacifics responsible for hauling prestige expresses between Glasgow Central and London Euston. In August 1966, when this photograph was taken, it still provided increasingly grubby locomotives (although No 76004 here looks surprisingly clean) for both goods and passenger workings, but this would not continue for much longer. Nevertheless, the site remains operational today, servicing electric and diesel traction. *Martin Jenkins / Online Transport Archive*

effects of the Industrial Revolution and the town's expanding trade with North America and the West Indies, which saw the population increase from 43,000 in 1780 to 120,000 by 1820. Dredging and improvements to the westerly-flowing Clyde allowed ambitious merchants and ship-owners to load and unload cargo. The wealth generated from the importation of cotton, tobacco and sugar led to the emergence of a modern progressive city with a central-area grid pattern of streets and an array of splendid public and private buildings. Gradually the riverbanks were swallowed up by miles of quays, acres of docks and large shipbuilding yards. Coupled with this was a growth in labour-intensive works, factories, foundries and forges. As a result Glasgow became one of the great workshops of the world and Scotland's major port of Empire.

Of the bridges spanning the river, the oldest dating from six centuries earlier, the most important was Glasgow Bridge, and the newest George V Bridge, opened in 1928. In the absence of bridges west of the city centre there were a variety of cross-river ferries, some centuries old and some later capable of transporting people and vehicles.

To combat appalling poverty and provide improved accommodation for the thousands pouring into the burgeoning city from the surrounding countryside, high-occupancy tenement buildings were built close to the river and the major industrial complexes. Between 1870 and 1900 the population rose from around 500,000 to 760,000. During this period several neighbouring burghs and districts were absorbed.

After World War 1 the population kept increasing, even though the city's heavy industrial base was already in decline, the sectarian divide was weakening, and there were increasing calls for improved, more spacious housing. In an attempt to improve living conditions Glasgow Corporation built municipal housing, having already taken control of sanitation, sewerage and water. It also assumed responsibility for gas and electricity supplies and opened parks, museums and galleries. The population topped the million mark when the burghs of Govan and Partick were annexed in 1912, and further additions were made in the 1930s.

The Industrial Revolution was fuelled by massive quantities of coal and an abundance of cheap labour, so the trans-shipment of coal to the Clyde, first by canal and later by rail, became of prime importance. Opened in 1831, the Gankirk & Glasgow Railway brought both coal and passengers into the city. As 'railway mania' took hold Glasgow became the focus for a vast complex of goods and passenger lines, the latter enabling some to live in the suburbs but work in the city, which eventually had four passenger termini in fairly close proximity. Coinciding with the opening of Queen Street, a Glasgow–Edinburgh service was inaugurated in 1842, and in 1848 through carriages were first run between Glasgow and London. Buchanan Street opened in 1849, to be followed by St Enoch in 1876 and Central in 1879. From 1871 passengers could also travel under the city centre in smoke-clogged tunnels. Complementing the many steam lines was the much cleaner 4ft-gauge, cable-operated underground railway, on which trains passed beneath the river at two points during their 6½-mile circular journey. Opened in 1896, the privately owned subway was acquired by the Corporation in 1922, electrified in 1935 and, much modernised, is still running today.

As the population expanded, so did the demand for public road transport. Glasgow's first horse-drawn tramway opened in 1872 to the unusual gauge of 4ft 7¾in, which enabled standard-gauge (4ft 8½in) goods wagons to run in parts of Govan over the same tracks. In 1894 the Corporation took over the operation of the tramways, and the first electric route opened in 1898. Eventually Glasgow had one of the most progressive tramways in the country, with a network of around 250 route miles, its tentacles of track and wires spread way beyond the city boundary into the counties of Dunbarton, Lanark and Renfrew. At one time or other Glasgow owned tramways in several neighbouring burghs. In 1922 it acquired the independent Airdrie & Coatbridge system, and one year later the Paisley District Tramways. Although some sections were abandoned as early as the 1920s Glasgow was at heart a tram city. Hundreds of comfortable, modern double-deckers were built between 1937 and 1954, extensions were opened, and plans existed for a postwar light-rail system with central-area subways. However, as part of a decision to electrify much of the suburban 'heavy' rail network the Corporation agreed to give up many of its out-of-boundary routes, buses — mainly from the nationalised companies — taking over. Then came the decision to scrap the trams, the last cars running in 1962. Although most were replaced by motor buses, between 1949 and 1958 a few routes had been converted to trolleybus operation, which in turn would be phased out by the end of 1967.

Corporation buses had first appeared on the scene in 1924, by which time private operators were already running into the city. In 1926 these companies were assigned specific termini, usually with on-street loading. By 1930 there were 1,300 private buses battling for limited street space with 220 Corporation buses and 1,100 trams. In later years central-area bus stations catered for the Scottish Bus Group, whose various subsidiaries operated into the city from the outer suburbs and beyond, but these termini offered little in the way of comfort or amenities, and there were strict regulations governing the operation of services within the city boundary. However, with the passing of the Corporation trams and trolleybuses the motor bus would ultimately reign supreme.

The photographs selected for inclusion in this book were all taken between 1949 and 1969. Each has been chosen to show something that no longer exists or has been radically altered; this may be a significant location, building or group of buildings, a type or make of road or rail vehicle, a ship or ferry, even an entire streetscape. The scenes are restricted to the area once served by the Corporation's extensive tram system, and it is the hope of both authors that their selection will revive memories of many 'bygone' aspects of this great city.

Acknowledgements

The authors would like to acknowledge in particular the extraordinary image-restoration work undertaken by Mike Eyre on a number of the older slides. They also wish to thank Mair and Andy McCann, for permission to use slides taken by John McCann, Seb Marshall, for permission to use slides taken by Prince Marshall, Peter Waller, for use of the colour negative taken by his father, Michael H. Waller, Richard Morant, for access to the G. W. Morant collection, Ray DeGroote, for sending his precious images across the Atlantic for scanning and digital enhancement, Graham Ewing, Brian Longworth, Hugh McAulay and David L. Thomson, for their invaluable assistance with the captions, and Maureen Campbell, for achieving computer-programming compatibility. Most of the copyright-holders have waived their royalty payments so that the monies can go to the Scottish Tramway & Transport Society (STTS) and Online Transport Archive (OTA), both of which organisations have also provided slides from their collections. Each author has donated his writing fee, one to the STTS and one to OTA, of which he is a trustee. OTA was established in 2000 to ensure that transport collections of slides, negatives and cine films are secured for posterity; the Archive (a UK registered charity) may be contacted at 8 Aughton Court, Church Road, Upton, Wirral, CH49 6JY. The STTS website is www.stts-glasgow.co.uk.

Bibliography

A Nostalgic Look at Glasgow's Trams since 1950 by G. H. Twidale and R. F. Mack (Silver Link Publishing, 1988)
Another Nostalgic Look at Glasgow's Trams since 1950 by Brian Patton (Silver Link Publishing, 1994)
An Illustrated History of Glasgow's Railways by W. A. C. Smith and Paul Anderson (Irwell Press, 1993)
Circles under the Clyde — A History of the Glasgow Underground by John Wright and Ian MacLean (Capital Transport, 1997)
Excursion Ships and Ferries by John S. Styring (Ian Allan, 1958)
Glasgow Buses by Stuart Little (STMS / Transport Publishing Company, 1990)
Glasgow Trams 40 Years On by Ian Stewart (STTS, 2002)
Glasgow Tram Services by David L. Thomson (STTS / Venture Publications, 2009)
Glasgow Tramway and Railway Rolling Stock by John A. M. Emslie (STMS, 1958)
Glasgow's Trolleybuses by Brian T. Deans (STMS, 1972)
Modern Tramway & Light Railway Review (various issues) (Ian Allan, 1962-73)
Paisley's Trams and Buses by A. W. Brotchie and R. L. Grieves (NB Traction, 1988)
abc British Railway Locomotives (Ian Allan, 1962)
Streets of Glasgow by Alan Millar (Ian Allan, 2004)
The Glasgow Tramcar by Ian Stewart (STMS, 1983 and 1994)
Tramways of Western Scotland by J. C. Gillham and R. J. S. Wiseman (LRTA, 2002)

Right: This 'bygone' tour begins, appropriately, on the Clyde at the Broomielaw, just west of George V Bridge. Older Glaswegians will recall that this was the embarkation point for steamers to Belfast until the service was discontinued in 1967. With their distinctive red, pale blue and black funnels, Burns & Laird Line ships operated both freight and passenger sailings to Ireland. Before the advent of budget air travel it was quite usual to take an overnight sailing to Belfast. Built in 1936 for this prestige service were two well-remembered vessels — the *Royal Ulsterman* seen here and her sister ship the *Royal Scotsman*. On occasions such as the Glasgow Fair or the Orange Walk in Belfast both were rostered to the appropriate port to meet demand. *Marcus Eavis / Online Transport Archive*

Below right: The sail downriver offered tantalising glimpses of ferries, docks, shipbuilding yards and associated industries. Star of this 1955 view is Burns & Laird's coaster *Lairdscraig*, also dating from 1936. *Richard and Joe Braun / Online Transport Archive*

A ¼-mile north of the Broomielaw is another iconic city-centre location, 'The Heilanman's Umbrella' — the tunnel-like span supporting Central station which once provided a social gathering place for Highlanders. This view towards the west side is instantly recognisable today, although the trams which once echoed beneath disappeared in 1962. No 1118 was one of 50 so-called 'Kilmarnock Bogie' cars introduced in 1928/9; these 68-seaters were for many years associated with the long, straight cross-city services 9 and 26 linking Clydebank to Bridgeton Cross and beyond. The only year the popular 'Five-Past-Eight' summer review at the Alhambra Theatre took advertising space on the trams, as seen on the dash panel, was 1955. The billing is (in order!): 'Jack Radcliffe, Jimmy Logan, Kenneth McKellar and Olga Gwynne'; the young choreographer and dancer was Lionel Blair, and the show was produced by Michael Mills, later Head of Comedy for BBC Television. *J. B. C. McCann / Online Transport Archive*

Right: A comedian recalled asking a visitor what he thought of Glasgow and receiving the reply "It'll be lovely when it is finished". In truth, Glasgow will never be finished and is in continual transition. This bygone tour now follows the north-west corridor through the industrial, heavily-populated neighbourhoods hugging the north bank of the Clyde formerly served by ferries, trams, buses and trains. In this view a postwar 'Cunarder' is loading just west of the Argyle Street/ Hope Street junction. Today this vista has totally changed. Gone are the low-rise shops to the right, replaced by a modern office block, whilst, opposite, the Grandfare building and the tenements beyond have given way to the dramatic façade of the Radisson Hotel. *Vernon Wood*

Below right: A short distance west of Central station is Anderston Cross, although everything in this view, except the buildings in the far distance, was swept away during the late 1960s in connection with construction of the Kingston Bridge and approaches to the Clydeside Expressway. Regular tram operation ceased on 1 September 1962, but for the next three days a special flat-fare service operated from Anderston Cross to Auchenshuggle. As the final car departed on 4 September 1962 the policeman on point duty stood smartly to attention, halted all other traffic, signalled the tram through and then saluted. There wasn't a dry eye on board! *D. E. Sinclair*

This 1959 view features a pair of 'puffers' berthed in Queen's Dock, constructed in 1880. Similar to the little vessels which serviced the West Highlands and Islands of Scotland until 1994 (and were immortalised in *The Tales of Para Handy*), *Turk* and *Slav* measured 66ft in length and 18ft across the beam, could carry up to 120 tons of coal and were able to negotiate locks on the Forth & Clyde and Crinan canals. Beyond, emerging from the tunnels leading to Queen Street Low Level on a test run, are a pair of three-car electric multiple-units (EMUs), soon to be known as 'Blue Trains'. Following the decision to electrify much of the city's suburban rail network using the 25kV overhead system many out-of-boundary Corporation tram services were replaced by buses, mostly from the nationalised companies. The dock site is now infilled and occupied by the Scottish Exhibition and Conference Centre (1985), its adjacent hotel and 'The Armadillo' auditorium. *Vernon Wood*

Just north of the former Queen's Dock is an open area surrounding the Kelvingrove Art Gallery and Museum (1901). Reopened in 2006 after restoration, the Galleries are a source of great civic pride, as were the Corporation's famous 'Coronation' trams, of which 152 were built at Coplawhill Works between 1937 and 1941. Nearing the end of its life, No 1284 is seen westbound on 1 June 1962. In the far distance are the old buildings of the Western Infirmary and, to the left of the Galleries, those of Glasgow University. On the right are examples of different types of 'street furniture' once found in similar clusters across the city. These included subterranean public conveniences, police boxes and telephone kiosks. In the days before mobile phones people often queued to make a call. The police boxes were used by beat policemen, who could be summoned by a roof-mounted flashing red light. The toilets were quaintly signed 'LAVATORY FOR GENTLEMEN'; there are not so many to be found today (lavatories, that is …). *Cedric Greenwood*

Above: The various ferries which once transported passengers and vehicles across the river have nearly all been superseded by bridges and tunnels, leaving just the heavily subsidised, pedestrian-only Renfrew Ferry, which survives today on a knife-edge. Until 1962 the crossing was operated by this chain-driven vessel, which conveyed vehicles and pedestrians across the 200yd width of river. Commissioned in 1952, it subsequently became a performance venue / restaurant and café bar and, named 'The Ferry', is berthed nowadays at Anderston Quay. In former times the ferry thronged with people going to and from work, and lines of vehicles often formed on both approaches. Until 1957 those disembarking on the Renfrew side could board a bus or tram towards Paisley, whilst on the north bank it was but a short walk to Dumbarton Road. At the time of the tramway closure the fare was 1d. *Brian Patton*

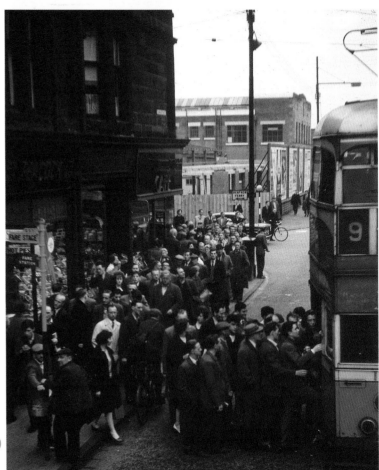

Right: Flanked for much of its length by high-density tenements and serving shipyards and factories, including major employers like Albion Motors and Singer, Dumbarton Road once supported an intensive service of buses and trams. The latter enjoyed a deserved reputation for swallowing up crowds, and at peak times there was nearly always another in sight. More than 70 people, of whom only a handful are women, are seen boarding a stone's throw from Renfrew Ferry (indicated by the sign on the lamp post) on 1 September 1962. Did any realise that the following day the familiar trams would be gone? (Note that the tram-stop pole has already been repainted from red to yellow in anticipation.) The road ahead shortly reached the independent Burgh of Clydebank, which, not to be outdone, held its own tramway farewell on 6 September 1962, two days after the final parade in Glasgow. *Ian Dunnett / Online Transport Archive*

The *Queen Elizabeth 2* was the last liner launched on the Clyde and the last to be built at John Brown's shipyard at Clydebank. During the previous weekend TS *Duchess of Hamilton* (1932-1970, featured) operated pre-launch cruises up to the slipway, and on the day itself, 20 September 1967, was joined by PS *Caledonia*. Although the river seems incredibly narrow at this point, additional space was provided opposite the shipyard by the mouth of the River Cart. However, it still required the combined skills of the various Clyde Navigation Trust tugboat captains to nudge the giant liner into position. Some eyebrows were raised when she was named 'Queen Elizabeth the Second'. Shortly before, a postbox bearing 'EⅡR' had been blown up. However, it was explained that 'the Second' applied to the ship and not the monarch, who in Scotland is Queen Elizabeth I. After a 40-year career, the *QE2* was to make an emotional farewell visit to her birthplace on 5 October 2008. *J. G. Parkinson / Online Transport Archive*

At peak times lines of extra trams came west each weekday conveying workers. Scheduled 'Shipyard Specials' from depots not normally associated with Dumbarton Road services usually displayed 'blank' number screens or had the indicator set between two service numbers, as seen on the 'Standard' ready to reverse at Clydebank crossover on 25 May 1955. In the foreground is Pullman bogie car No 1089 of 1926. Built by the Corporation and designed to compete with bus operators by offering a fast, comfortable ride on longer inter-urban services, this experimental car proved operationally unsuccessful, spending its latter years as a 'crush-loader' from Partick depot; surviving until 1961, it was nicknamed by shipyard workers as 'Wee Baldy' (because there was nothing on top) and as 'Baillie Burt's car' (after the Tramways Convenor responsible for its introduction). The motorman was often the depot shop steward, who, owing to his other commitments, was allocated a restricted rush-hour duty. The car is now preserved. *Ray DeGroote / Online Transport Archive*

Half a mile further west was a swing bridge over the Forth & Clyde Canal. When this replaced an earlier structure in 1915 Glasgow trams were extended to Dalmuir West, linking with the Dumbarton Burgh & County Tramways, which were cut back to the same point. Until the abandonment of the Dumbarton system in 1928 thousands of Glaswegians changed trams here to travel to the shores of Loch Lomond. In September 1959 the bridge closed for repairs, and it was feared that trams would be permanently relegated to the east side. When it reopened, 11 months later, the sceptics were proved wrong, and trams once again ran the extra ½ mile to Dalmuir West. This photograph, taken from the canal bank on 31 August 1962, shows the control cabin and the gantries supporting the overhead wires. Catch points were located on either side to divert oncoming trams away from the bridge when opened. The canal closed in 1963 but reopened for leisure traffic in 2002. *Marcus Eavis / Online Transport Archive*

North-west of Dalmuir another canal crossing prevented trams from reaching nearby postwar housing developments, which were served instead by buses, as apparent from this photograph, taken on 31 May 1959. Glasgow's last major tramway extension, from Knightswood Cross to Blairdardie (opened on 31 July 1949), ended on the east side of the canal, where round-dash 'Standard' No 302 is seen waiting to reverse. This was the limit of a two-mile stretch of private tramway track along Great Western Road used by service 30.

Postwar plans submitted by Transport Manager E. R. L. Fitzpayne to upgrade the tram system with more reserved tracks, subways and single-deckers were rejected. Few modern cars traversed the Great Western Road reservation, as only 'Standards' were able to negotiate the tight curves at Parkhead Cross used by services 1 and 30. Today there is considerably more traffic at this point, and the median strip ideal for 'rapid transit' has been grassed over. *Marcus Eavis / Online Transport Archive*

The former Botanic Gardens station (1896) on the Glasgow Central Railway's line to Maryhill formed an impressive backdrop to the junction of Great Western Road with Byres Road and Queen Margaret Drive. Although this line carried passenger trains until 1959 and freight until 1964 the station closed in 1939; it was subsequently destroyed by fire (in 1970), but most of the tunnels in the West End are still extant, albeit derelict. Great Western Road was used by several long-distance bus services entering the city. In the distance is a Maudslay coach of David MacBrayne, nearing the end of its long journey from Campbeltown, whilst the black-and-white coach nearer the camera is a Plaxton-bodied Dennis belonging to Garelochhead Motor Services. The patching of the road surface indicates where the tram tracks into Byres Road used to be. Hex-dash 'Standard' No 22 is now preserved at the National Tramway Museum at Crich, Derbyshire, but in 1988 briefly returned home as one of five cars to operate on a specially built tram line in connection with the city's Garden Festival. *J. J. W. Richards*

In bygone times it was claimed that the only route into Glasgow to avoid the slum areas was Great Western Road, which even at its inner end was graced by Victorian terraces with access roads and private gardens. In June 1959 a 'Standard' is seen passing Buckingham Terrace on service 10 (Kelvinside–London Road), which was withdrawn without replacement a year later. Approximately 1,000 'Standards' were built, nearly all by the Corporation, between 1898 and 1924; they encompassed two basic types — older round-dash and newer hex-dash — although over the years all were completely enclosed and upgraded with new trucks and motors. Further to the west, plans to build an arterial road by removing the tree-lined boulevards and flanking terraces in the quest to speed up traffic flows were shouted down, and this incipient act of municipal vandalism was never perpetrated. One messes with the articulate West End at one's peril! *A. S. Clayton / Online Transport Archive*

Before the age of digital photography it was difficult to capture scenes like this, for early colour-slide film was slow and preferred bright sunshine. It took more than fog and snow to stop the trams from running, and, judging by the lack of people, the uncleared pavements and the fact that the snow has not yet been pounded into slush, this was probably a Sunday morning. Making its way cautiously along Great Western Road just before the descent to Kelvinbridge, the 'Standard', on service 10, is cautiously following a works car, the crew of which are probably keeping an eye on the effects of weather, ensuring that as near-normal a service as possible is maintained. In its heyday the extensive tram system was supported by a fleet of at least 30 departmental vehicles; these tended to be nocturnal and carried out a range of tasks including permanent-way duties, weed-killing, water-spraying and delivering dried sand to depots. The arcing between the bow collector and the overhead was caused by periodic loss of contact due to frost or ice forming on the wire. *D. E. Sinclair*

Left: Glasgow's most northerly tram terminus was in the Burgh of Milngavie. From here the long cross-city service 29 to Broomhouse became one of the mainstays for 46 trams purchased from Liverpool Corporation during 1953/4. Just south of Milngavie terminus was the site of the Bennie Railplane test track erected in 1930, the elevated structure being visible to the right in the first two of views recorded in late May 1955 on the 3½-mile extension from Maryhill (opened in 1934). George Bennie, the inventor of this form of monorail with a carriage shaped like an aeroplane fuselage but with a propeller at each end, failed to convince investors. The track was removed along with the structure by the early 1960s. *Ray DeGroote / Online Transport Archive*

Left: In the second view another ex-Liverpool car passes Bearsden (tramway) substation. Such structures were normally basic or utilitarian in appearance, but this one, in keeping with the area, was constructed of red sandstone. It survives as Kessington Community Hall, although one suspects that few of today's patrons know of its previous use, which ceased when service 29 was finally abandoned. *Ray DeGroote / Online Transport Archive*

Right: Closer into town, until June 1961, trams again encountered the Forth & Clyde Canal high above Bilsland Drive on an aqueduct built in 1879. Inbound cars faced a steady descent from Ruchill, but the danger lay in tackling a sharp bend immediately before the portal. On three occasions over the years runaways came to grief here, two cars being write-offs and the third requiring extensive rebuilding. Each had toppled over at the curve and come to rest against the stone wall seen here. *D. Norman / Online Transport Archive*

Below: The second view emphasises the tight bend (the tracks hugging the kerb) and the poor visibility on the opposite side of the aqueduct. When trolley poles were replaced by bow collectors these had especially shallow contact balance rods on their plates, enabling them to be pressed down almost flat in order to pass under this and similar bridges. After negotiating the tight bend in the foreground trams approached the junction with Maryhill Road. Advertisements for rival alcoholic beverages offer a choice of Usher's Amber Ale, Fowler's 'Wee Heavy' or McEwan's — 'The best buy in beer'. *A. S. Clayton / Online Transport Archive*

St George's Cross is today but a shadow of its former self, having been downgraded from a busy commercial junction by the construction of ramps from the adjacent M8 motorway. Formerly it was a hectic five-way intersection between Great Western Road, Maryhill Road and New City Road, with St George's Road crossing from south to north. With up to nine tram services clattering through, the points and crossings took a heavy pounding for nearly 20 hours a day. Even though the junction was to be abandoned in October 1961 its poor overall condition led to its complete renewal as late as October 1959. The layout was pre-fabricated at the Barrland Street Permanent Way Yard, like some massive model railway to a scale of 12in to the foot. The Transport Department chose the renewal date very carefully to coincide with the night the clocks went back, gaining an extra hour, and the task was completed with minutes to spare before arrival of the first service tram — no over-running possessions in those days! The aerial view gives some idea of the complicated track configuration.
Vernon Wood; D. E. Sinclair

Right: By the late 1960s Glasgow was a city in transition. This photograph was taken at Charing Cross in 1968 when the area was being excavated for the new M8 motorway, which burrowed underneath. During the construction buses were diverted round the craters and spoil heaps. Among the many properties razed to the ground was the Grand Hotel (1880); this was once owned by the Co-op, and it would be fair to say that those who objected to its demolition probably never used it. The area to the north-west of Charing Cross is Glasgow's equivalent of Edinburgh's New Town and has survived intact. *Ian Stewart*

Below right: A short distance south-east of Charing Cross is Bothwell Street, where the solid Victorian edifices seen here in 1959, including the majestic YMCA, later gave way to glass-and-concrete structures which have themselves now been replaced by more impressive construction. Of the two trams passing Douglas Street crossover, No 1393 was one of six replacement 'Coronations' built in 1954 on trucks salvaged from a Liverpool depot fire (and, ironically, would itself be consumed in the Dalmarnock depot fire of March 1961, when 50 trams were lost). In the background a window-cleaner perches precariously on a second-floor ledge. What would today's Health & Safety Executive have to say? *E. C. Bennett and Martin Jenkins / Online Transport Archive*

Left: The first of two central locations which are now virtually unrecognisable features a 'Coronation' on service 23 at the north end of Cambridge Street near its junction with New City Road, none of which survives today; even the road pattern has altered. The building to the right, adorned with advertising for Cadbury's, was at the edge of Garnethill, and the low building on the bend, behind the Alexander's Leyland bus, belonged to Gibbs, whose emporium specialised in the sale of 'pianofortes'. When this photograph was taken in 1959 the area was a base for theatrical landladies, the main advantage being proximity to the city's principal theatres. Accommodation was homely, the landladies being (generally) motherly and prepared to deal with their guests' odd working hours. *E. C. Bennett and Martin Jenkins / Online Transport Archive*

Left: Recorded on 26 May 1967, this view west along Cowcaddens from the top of West Nile Street features Crossley-bodied BUT trolleybus TB106 bound for Clarkston on route 105. The property on the left was subsequently demolished to make way for an extension of Scottish Television's original headquarters, opposite which is today the School of Piping (bagpipes, not plumbing), and the tenements seen on the right have been replaced by prestige apartments. *Mike Russell*

Springburn once had four world-renowned, labour-intensive locomotive-building works, but by the early 1960s these were in terminal decline, as were its trams, the last services (18/18A) operating on 3 June 1961. A week before, 'Coronation' No 1195 was photographed flanked by a pair of Austin FX3 taxis outside The Boundary public house in Hawthorn Street. The blackened tenements on Springburn Road would soon be demolished.

In the decades that followed, planners effectively ripped the heart out of this community by driving a new road through the district. As if to avoid embarrassment, traffic now speeds through as quickly as possible, and what remains bears little comparison with the Springburn of old, as featured in the evocative writings of the late Molly Weir. *Anthony Henry*

This spectacular overview of the Corporation-owned Pinkston Power Station and the surrounding railways dates from 1 October 1956. The sustained climb from Queen Street station to the summit at Cowlairs had a maximum gradient of 1 in 41½, requiring the use of banking engines, hence the smoke visible in the distance as 'A4' Pacific No 60004 *William Whitelaw* pounds away from the tunnel. The train is the 11am to Edinburgh Waverley, comprising a rake of former LNER carriages in the contemporary livery of carmine and cream, known to some as 'blood and custard' (and quite different from the colours used today by Strathclyde Passenger Transport). Within the year steam was replaced on this service by six-car 'Inter-City' DMUs. Fuelled by locally produced coal (note the ex-North British Railway 0-6-0 goods engine heading a line of empty wagons away from the yard), the power station provided cheap electricity for the trams, trolleybuses and subway, but a transfer of ownership to the nationalised Electricity Board in 1958 effectively spelt the end for the trams and trolleybuses.
J. G. Todd / Online Transport Archive

The stretch of Springburn Road seen here in 1955 now leads to the expressway linking the Townhead interchange on the M8 to a point north of Springburn but had earlier formed part of Glasgow's first, experimental electric tram route, opened in 1898 between Mitchell Street and Springburn. To serve this a small power station and depot were built at Keppochhill Road, the depot later being replaced by the much larger facility at Possilpark, home to 'Standard' No 57 of 1921. Behind the tram are St Rollox Church and Sighthill Cemetery, while the 'Coronation' on the right, pursued by an Albion CX3 lorry laden with beer barrels, is passing the St Rollox Works of the former Caledonian Railway, known affectionately as the 'Caley'. Today Springburn Works is the only remnant of the railway industry still functioning in this area; operated by Railcare, it concentrates on repair and refurbishment work. *J. B. C. McCann / Online Transport Archive*

With Castle Street in the background, the late-evening sun catches 'Coronation' No 1144 in Monkland Street at its junction with Parliamentary Road on 22 August 1959. As part of a one-way traffic flow introduced in 1946, trams heading east to Alexandra Parade were re-routed along Parliamentary Road (left); westbound they continued to use Monkland Street, where the former eastbound track was retained to reach a crossover used by short workings, especially during peak hours. Taking advantage of the revised traffic arrangements is an Alexander's coach, parked on the wrong side of the road to load passengers for a private hire. Today this once thriving neighbourhood has disappeared. During the 1970s the tenements, local shops, warehouses, railway properties, Dundas Street bus station, bus-parking areas with rubble surfaces and the most primitive departure-point of all, used by David MacBrayne's buses to Campbeltown, were all swept away for the M8 Townhead interchange. *D. G. Clarke*

Right: The long-gone Parliamentary Road tenements can be seen in this view of Dundas Street bus station (1944). Although David Lawson had been taken over by W. Alexander & Sons in 1936 it continued to trade under its own name until 1961, despite its vehicles' being numbered in the Alexander series and fitted with the same style of cast aluminium fleet-number and garage-allocation plates. G14, a 35-seater Duple-bodied Guy Arab of 1947, was photographed on 18 September 1961, just months after Alexander, with its fleet of 2,000 buses, had been split into the three — Midland, Fife and Northern. As a result Lawson's red and cream would give way to the blue-based Midland livery. *Ian Dunnett / Online Transport Archive*

Below right: Used by routes serving the north of the city, nearby Killermont Street bus station (1934-76) had one main exit. Pictured emerging into Buchanan Street through the portal in 1961 bound for Cumbernauld New Town is Alexander (Midland) Leyland PD3 MRB248. Although fitted with a 67-seat Alexander body it had started life as a single-decker coach in 1952. As per Scottish Bus Group practice, the paper stickers in the lower-deck front window enhance (but sometimes contradicted) the destination display. All trace of this site has since vanished, cleared to make way for the Park Inn, the Royal Concert Hall, Concert Square and multi-storey car parks. *Brian Patton*

A major north–south artery, Renfield Street once carried substantial tram traffic. In rush hours there was a car every 12½ seconds on this steep section between Sauchiehall Street and St Vincent Street, where in May 1959 a northbound service 1 is seen bound for Yoker, while No 334 heads south for Mosspark. After a long absence Corporation buses had reappeared on tram-replacement services in 1957. These buildings still survive, and most have benefited from stone cleaning and refurbishment. Only the Odeon Cinema presents a sorry sight. Originally the Paramount (1934), it was the last of Glasgow's prewar 'super cinemas'. Victim of the multiplex cinemas, usually out of town or able to offer adjacent car parking, it has been boarded up for some years while a future is planned for this art-deco building. In a bid to improve traffic flows, Renfield Street has now been made one-way southbound, although in today's peak-hour traffic it can still take an hour to travel by this route from Renfrew Street to Glasgow Bridge! *Marcus Eavis / Online Transport Archive*

Right: The first of two photographs taken at the east end of St Vincent Street. The virtual absence of traffic highlights the contour of the street, with the tram tracks stopping about halfway up the slope beyond Hope Street, overlooked by the spire of the Gaelic Church in the distance. Pictured having just swung left from West Nile Street, bound for George Square on service 105 (Queen's Cross–Clarkston) on 16 June 1957, is Daimler trolleybus TD18, with London Transport-style bodywork. All the buildings in the foreground have been retained and refurbished, although further up the hill some new high-specification office blocks have been built in recent years. *Marcus Eavis / Online Transport Archive*

Below right: The second view, recorded six years earlier, features 'Standard' tram No 742 on service 11 (Milngavie–Sinclair Drive), destined to be replaced in July 1951 — partly by the strengthening of other tram services and partly by new motor-bus service 43. Dating from 1900, No 742 would be withdrawn in 1955. External advertising on trams began only in 1950. The lower destination indicator features a spelling howler in 'Eglington Toll' (perpetuated today by Network Rail), while the British Road Services Fordson lorry on the right displays the same 'starved lion' logo used at the time by British Railways. *C. Carter*

Laid out in 1781, the city's most prominent open space is George Square, with its statues and grand civic and commercial buildings, most surviving today. This photograph, dating from July 1955, shows the west side at its junction with Queen Street and focuses on the array of vehicles to be seen when all the roads were still two-way. With the traffic lights switched off, a policeman on 'points' duty tries to control the traffic as an early split-screen Morris Minor stands alongside tram No 442 heading a line of 'Standards' waiting to turn into St Vincent Place. Behind is one of the Corporation's

Albion Venturer CX19 motor buses, on service 35; delivered in 1947, these featured very upright bodywork by Charles Roberts. Heading in the opposite direction is a British Railways pick-up truck, with canvas hood, making for Queen Street Station, next to the North British (nowadays Millennium) Hotel. In this view the station's glass roofing is still coated with blackout paint and years of accumulated soot and grime. The arch is no longer visible from this point, having been obscured since the 1970s by an extension to the hotel.
Richard and Joe Braun / Online Transport Archive.

Glasgow's trolleybus fleet was small compared with the trams, yet with a maximum of 195 vehicles it became the third largest in the UK. Always keen to support Scottish industries, in 1953 the Corporation purchased five Sunbeams (TG1-5) with bodywork by Alexander, of which TG1 was fitted initially with a Corporation-designed single trolley split to accommodate twin trolley heads. Intended to reduce de-wiring, it proved unsuccessful. This rare view features the 62-seater in Queen Street, with trolley poles pulled down, there being no overhead wiring at this location; in all probability it was Remembrance Sunday, when the area around the George Square cenotaph was closed to traffic and the 105 trolleybuses were diverted along Ingram Street to Queen Street, using battery power, before turning into St Vincent Place and regaining the traction wiring. The people waiting to cross are clearly in their 'Sunday best'.
P. J. Marshall

Left: In 1949 trolleybuses replaced High Street tram service 2. Dominating this view is Provand's Lordship, the last surviving mediæval building in this ancient thoroughfare. Formerly part of St Nicholas's Hospital and passed to the City Museums in 1978, it looks across towards the 800-year-old Glasgow Cathedral and is itself overlooked by the bulk of the Royal Infirmary. The photograph was taken at 8.57am on 29 April 1966, the last day trolleybuses used High Street. Seen having negotiated the Cathedral Street turning-circle prior to heading south into Castle Street, TB20 was one of 34 BUT 9641Ts with Metro-Cammell bodies delivered during 1949/50. *Mike Russell*

Right: The second view of High Street, recorded in 1959, features the junction with Gallowgate. Waiting to be waved across *en route* to Hampden garage is TBS2, one of 10 BUT RETB1s delivered during 1953 with East Lancs bodies. The 'standee' windows were part of a design to accommodate 40 standing and 27 seated passengers. Originally equipped for passenger flow with seated conductor and rear-loading and centre-exit doors, all were later rebuilt as 36-seaters with rear entrance removed, and withdrawn in 1964. Beyond the Central SMT Bristol Lodekka and easily identifiable by the large illuminated sign can be seen Bow's furniture store — premises now occupied by 'The Bed Shed'. *P. J. Marshall*

Only a short distance from the Cathedral and Provand's Lordship was the industrial East End, with its poorer working-class neighbourhoods. In this atmospheric scene, recorded in Dennistoun at the junction of Duke Street with Cumbernauld Road in June 1959, the men wear cloth caps, while the shops include a hairdresser's — complete with barber's pole — a bank, a fireplace showroom and a chemist's. Although the granite setts look neglected, there is a complete absence of litter. Note also the 'NO WAITING' signs, which would soon give way to yellow lines. Working service 30, car No 17 will continue east into the haze surrounding the giant Beardmore's steelworks; it was said that those living in the vicinity took their babies out in their prams for a cough. The tracks to the right connected with Alexandra Parade and were last regularly used in June 1958, when service 7 was replaced by trolleybus service 106. Both modes were housed at Dennistoun depot, immediately behind the camera. Unloved by motorists, the granite setts had lasting qualities sadly lacking in today's potholed roads and are now much sought after for hard landscaping.
E. C. Bennett and Martin Jenkins / Online Transport Archive

Left: Deep in the East End were the heavily used tramway junctions at Parkhead Cross, a significant local shopping and employment centre. In the first of two views car No 751 of 1900, having emerged from the gloom of the distant steelworks, is seen on the curve from Duke Street into Gallowgate, the tight radius having prevented the use of modern bogie cars, while preparing to turn left is a Triumph Mayflower. Until replaced by buses in March 1960, services 1 and 30 were the last routes in the UK worked entirely by traditional four-wheel trams, the basic turnout requiring 45 vehicles. *P. J. Marshall*

Below: Replacement of the 1 and 30 led to closure and demolition of the control tower on the right of this photograph, taken in June 1959. From within this lofty perch a pointsman set the correct road for cars using the five-way junction. The ex-Liverpool cars, confined to services 15 and 29, were all withdrawn by 1960. Although Westmuir Street remains largely unchanged, local shops were affected by the Forge Shopping Centre, opened on the site of the former steelworks. Hopes for further regeneration rest with the 2014 Commonwealth Games. *E. C. Bennett and Martin Jenkins / Online Transport Archive*

Right: Until 1958 Parkhead was connected with outlying housing schemes to the north-east by independent bus operator Lowland Motorways. This scene, recorded in Shettleston Road in 1957, features No 38 outside John Anderson's somewhat shabby 'boot and shoe repair factory.' In the company's livery of two-tone green with St Andrew's Cross on the side, this ex-London Transport Cravens-bodied AEC Regent (RT), dating from 1949, was bound for Barlanark on service A. Just visible on the right is a BR Scammell 'mechanical horse'. *G. W Morant*

Below right: When Lowland was acquired by Scottish Omnibuses (formerly SMT) in 1958 its fleet comprised some 36 double- and single-deckers, Among the former were two prewar Leyland TD5s, of which this example, acquired from East Yorkshire, had been rebodied by Eastern Coach Works in 1948 with a distinctive arched roof, enabling it to pass beneath the mediæval North Bar in Beverley. Bringing up the rear is a more typical Bristol Lodekka, purchased new by Scottish Omnibuses in 1958.The pale-green livery soon gave way to a darker 'Lothian' green, and the 'SMT' fleetname eventually became 'Eastern Scottish'. *Ian Dunnett / Online Transport Archive*

Glasgow's most impressive stretch of private tramway track lay outside the city boundary, between Baillieston and Langloan. The 2¼ miles of roadside reservation, with super-elevated curves, opened in 1923 and created a high-speed link with the 3½-mile route of the erstwhile Airdrie & Coatbridge Tramways Co, acquired by Glasgow the year before, along with all 15 cars. After completion of the new link the former A&C line was completely rebuilt, with double track throughout, although the depot at Coatbridge was

retained and supplied trams for a 'local' between Airdrie and Langloan as well as some for the 12-mile Airdrie–Glasgow inter-urban service. Here two 'Coronations' pass at speed at Drumpark in May 1955. Both retain original features, although No 1209 has had additional grilles inserted above the platform doors in an attempt to improve ventilation. Tramway operation east of Baillieston ended without replacement in November 1956. *Ray DeGroote / Online Transport Archive*

Serving the then steel towns of Airdrie and Coatbridge was Baxter's, an independent operator with a well-maintained fleet of around 50 buses and coaches. The distinctive blue-and-grey livery, coupled with good service record, guaranteed customer loyalty. This photograph of Massey-bodied Leyland PD2 No 66, dating from 1957, was taken in Airdrie in August 1961, 16 months before the company was taken over by SMT. When that happened the new operator committed a major gaffe by starting to repaint Baxter's vehicles in the pale-green 'Scottish' livery, thus forfeiting customer goodwill at a (brush) stroke. After some months the policy was reversed, and SMT even repainted some of its own existing and, later, new vehicles in Baxter colours. Regrettably the majority of today's large corporate operators seem unable to learn this lesson, resulting in a situation whereby local identity has been wiped out and identical buses fill the streets of Glasgow, Aberdeen and Edinburgh. *R. L. Wilson / Online Transport Archive*

The Airdrie tram terminus was well beyond the town centre, further east into Lanarkshire. At one time it was 200 yards beyond the two trams featured here, which resulted in generally empty trams' running the gauntlet across the (even then) busy A73 trunk road, to no obvious purpose. 'Standard' tram No 20 of 1922 was allocated to the small depot in Coatbridge and is pictured operating the 'Airdrie local' service from Langloan, west of Coatbridge, to Airdrie; cars on this service normally displayed no service number at all or had the screen set to show '15' over '23'. The 'Coronation' tram to the rear is awaiting its 59min return through journey into Glasgow three months before closure in 1956, the fare at this time being 6d (2½p). Note the advertisement hoardings mounted on the redundant abutment for the former railway bridge carrying the freight-only line serving Calderbank Steelworks. *D. G. Clarke*

A few miles south-west of Coatbridge is Broomhouse. Here trams terminated close to a crematorium and Calderpark Zoo, this location having become the eastern extremity of service 29 when a 2-mile section to Uddingston was abandoned in 1948. Although built to the same gauge there was no physical connection at Uddingston with the sprawling Lanarkshire Tramways Co system, abandoned during the early 1930s. The sign for the zoo (closed in 2003) can be seen in the trees behind the ex-Liverpool 'Streamliner' standing at the terminus on 20 June 1957. Built during 1936/7, these cars were not as robust as their Glasgow contemporaries, although one was later preserved by students from Liverpool University. In 1960 service 29 would be cut back to the city boundary at Tollcross, and before construction of the M74 motorway this evident backwater at Broomhouse would become an extremely busy part of the main A74 trunk road from Glasgow to Carlisle. *Marcus Eavis / Online Transport Archive*

Back to Parkhead for a late-1950s scene at the bus garage. Highlighting the Transport Department's commitment to use local firms whenever possible, all but three of the 19 buses on view had locally built bodies and chassis. Always an admirer of Albion Motors (motto: 'Sure as the Sunrise'), Glasgow built up the UK's largest fleet of this chassis make before the Scotstoun-based firm was taken over by Leyland in 1951. In bygone times Parkhead was very much an Albion garage, the last examples surviving until 1964. Most buses in this line-up are still in the traditional Corporation livery but have had their 'via' destination apertures overpainted, to save expenditure on linen. The three Albion Venturers nearest the camera are of type CX37, with bodywork by Brockhouse of Clydebank and Croft of Gallowgate, whilst examples furthest away had bodies by Scottish Aviation of Prestwick. Note that the surrounding buildings have yet to sprout television aerials.
P. J. Marshall

Right: South-west of Parkhead, on the south bank of the Clyde, is the Royal Burgh of Rutherglen. This photograph was taken in September 1961 on the railway bridge at the south end of Farmeloan Road. Working to Burnside on tram-replacement service 18 (the only instance latterly where the same number was used) is A359, one of 89 AEC Regent Vs with forward-entrance Alexander bodies, delivered during the period 1960-2. The public disliked their spartan interiors, and the buses soon displayed structural inadequacies. *Ian Dunnett / Online Transport Archive*

Below: Trolleybuses served Rutherglen for just 11 years. This view was recorded at the east end of Main Street on 29 April 1966, the final day of trolleybus service 101. Waiting to negotiate the anti-clockwise terminal loop is one of the original batch of 34 three-axle BUTs with MCW bodies delivered in 1949. The similarity of the Town Hall (background) to that at Renfrew must have confused the Luftwaffe crews who tried to bomb Rutherglen in 1941, presumably in the belief that they were over Renfrew and on their way to Clydebank. *Mike Russell*

Roughly midway between Rutherglen's Main Street and Dalmarnock Bridge is Farme Cross. Most of the line to Cambuslang (left) was abandoned in 1956, but trams continued to Burnside until 1961. Heading citywards in May 1955 is No 1120, one of 30 'Kilmarnock Bogie' cars with bodywork by Hurst Nelson of Motherwell and known officially as 'Standard Double Bogie' cars. The last of these 68-seaters was withdrawn in 1961. None of the buildings featured here survive. On the corner is one of the ubiquitous Co-op stores. In the days before frozen food and freezers fresh deliveries were made six days a week, but there was no Sunday trading. Hard at work are a variety of delivery vans including, parked at the kerb, a Co-op Albion with full-fronted body, while balancing on a second-storey ledge is yet another intrepid window-cleaner. At a time when soot and smoke filled the air it must have taken plenty of elbow grease to keep windows sparkling. *Ray DeGroote / Online Transport Archive*

On 4 September 1962 some 250,000 people, determined to give the trams a rousing send-off, lined the route of the 'last tram' procession. Befitting Britain's last 'big city' system, this was a memorable occasion, a parade of 20 cars carrying invited guests and balloted members of the public. Included were some trams superbly restored at Coplawhill, each representing a different epoch. Round-dash 'Standard' No 779 of 1900 was restored to 1908 condition, complete with open platforms and balconies, and painted as a 'red' car, recalling the days when services were identified by colours. The cavalcade progressed from Dalmarnock depot through the city centre to Coplawhill, this evocative scene being recorded in Dalmarnock Road, on the approach to Bridgeton Cross; 20 minutes later, before the one-way journey had been completed, the skies darkened ominously, heralding a torrential downpour that overwhelmed drains and engulfed trams and spectators alike. Seven of the trams were destined to remain in Glasgow, forming the basis of a transport museum; two others went to the National Tramway Museum in Derbyshire, while yet another was exported to the USA and can today be found at the Seashore Trolley Museum in Maine.
A. J. Douglas

Like Parkhead, Bridgeton Cross was another busy junction where a control tower played a key part in keeping heavily loaded trams, represented here by a 'Cunarder' and a 'Coronation', on the move. Heading east along London Road, they either went straight on past the Olympia Cinema (towards Auchenshuggle) or slewed south, where they immediately encountered a three-way junction, tracks leading variously hard right into James Street (with Glasgow Green in the distance), straight on down Main Street, Bridgeton (towards Rutherglen Bridge), and left along Dalmarnock Road (towards Dalmarnock Bridge and Farme Cross). The switching of points between these three roads was controlled from the cabin, but this was demolished after the James Street service (7) was converted to trolleybus (106) in June 1958. Behind the police box and the three policemen in this scene from June 1962 is the cast-iron 'Bridgeton Umbrella', built in 1875 by the Sun Foundry to 'shelter the unemployed', while mounted on the striped lamp-post is a multi-coloured sign giving colour-coded directions for lorry drivers heading for the various docks. The 'Umbrella' still stands today, but Bridgeton Cross is now by-passed by most through traffic. *Cedric Greenwood*

Until 1962 Glasgow Cross, in the city centre, was a significant tramway junction with Gallowgate (left) and London Road (right), both of which saw intensive services. In this view, recorded in 1959, the conductor of 'Standard' 75 prepares to 'flip the bow' as his tram reverses on a short working to Parkhead Cross. Interestingly the word 'Cross' is abbreviated on the destination indicator of No 75 but appears in full on eastbound 'Coronation' No 1251. This location remains easily recognisable today, and all of these buildings survive, most notably Tolbooth Steeple (1626), the last remnant of a former Town Hall and prison, and the solid-looking Mercat Building (right), dating from 1922. However, Glasgow Cross station (1896), occupying the central island behind No 1251, closed in 1964 along with the smoke-filled low-level railway running beneath Argyle Street. Thereafter the line remained unused until reopened in 1979 as the electrified Argyle Line, reached by way of a new station located within the shopping precinct west of Stockwell Street.
P. J. Marshall

Left: The worst central bus terminus, with no shelters and no pavements, was a cluster of stances adjacent to the wharves on Clyde Street, used by Western SMT and until 1951 by Youngs' Bus Service of Paisley. This Northern Counties-bodied Leyland PD2/1, delivered new to Youngs' in 1949, had become part of the Western fleet when Youngs' was taken over in 1951 and was destined to remain in front-line service until 1967. The 'J' fleet-number prefix denoted allocation to Johnstone garage, while the 'Policies' in the destination refers not to insurance documents but to the lands or estate of Johnstone Castle. In the foreground are the photographer's parents, his mother laden with shopping bags. Since this view was recorded in 1961 the dockside buildings have all gone, and the riverbank has been landscaped. *Brian Patton*

Below left: About to cross Victoria Bridge (rebuilt in 1854) southbound is TD20, one of 30 Metro-Cammell-bodied Daimler CTM6s in service from 1950 to 1964. Pictured in October 1956, it retains its original livery save for the addition of a green roof, the original cream having swiftly become stained with grease and graphite dropping from the trolley heads. On the left side of Stockwell Street (background) and just south of the bridge leading to St Enoch station is the Metropole Theatre, destined to burn down in 1961. Artists Harry Lauder and Jimmy Logan started their careers here, and Stanley, son of Manager Arthur Jefferson, later changed his name to Stan Laurel, of Laurel & Hardy fame. *J. G. Todd / Online Transport Archive*

The main South Side coverage begins at Gorbals Cross on 26 May 1967, shortly before the rest of this public space (1872) disappeared, the drinking fountain surmounted by a cast-iron pagoda and clock having already gone. The island refuge supports a 'phone box and a subterranean gentlemen's lavatory, desperation probably providing the adrenaline to run the gauntlet through the traffic. In trolleybus days this was a major intersection, the 106 running east–west and the 105 and 107 north–south, but 12 hours after this photograph was taken Glasgow's trolleybuses passed into history. Compared with that of the trams, their demise went largely unnoticed. By the end all remaining vehicles, among them TB70, were from a large batch of Crossley-bodied BUT 9613Ts delivered during 1957/8. As part of an ongoing transformation much of the redevelopment of this area has itself given way to the creation of the 'New Gorbals'. *Mike Russell*

Less than a mile south-west from Gorbals Cross is Eglinton Toll. In 1946 this complicated junction, also with control tower for the trams, was simplified by erection of the barrier just out of view (left). Trams continued to reach Coplawhill Works via Eglinton Street (left) until 1962, whilst trolleybuses on service 107 continued on the east side of the barrier until 1967. This last-day view, recorded at 10.41am on 25 February, features TB121; in the latter-day spray-painted livery, this was one of the short-lived BUTs delivered only nine years earlier. The 107 had been introduced in 1958 following representations from shopkeepers on Victoria Road, who demanded restoration of a direct link lost when the trolleybuses (which had replaced tram service 5) were re-routed via Cathcart Road. The barrier and the distinctive wedge-shaped St Andrew's Cross building, complete with the Star Bar and its art-deco exterior, survive today, but the tenements in Eglinton Street succumbed years ago. *Mike Russell*

A short distance south-west of Eglinton Toll were Coplawhill Car Works and its associated permanent-way yard in Barrland Street, from which was recorded on 7 April 1958 this view of Class 2F 0-6-0 No 57271, one of the celebrated 'Standard Goods' locomotives designed by Dugald Drummond for the Caledonian Railway and introduced from 1883. Hauling just a guard's van, it is probably returning to shed after working a pick-up freight serving various yards, many of which handled domestic coal supplies. The timber yard and the Maxwell Road gas-holder are still extant, but the chimney stack and most of the industrial buildings have gone. The track layout just beyond Pollokshields East station has been greatly simplified and is used nowadays by suburban EMUs on the Cathcart Circle and the Neilston and Newton lines and by DMUs to East Kilbride and Kilmarnock. *Paul de Beer / Online Transport Archive*

Many of the more prosperous South Side suburbs have altered little during the past 50 years. It was claimed that cars for former 'white' service 3 were well kept to please prominent councillors who lived along the route. In 1923 this service was extended along Mosspark Boulevard to serve a new, well-laid-out Corporation housing estate, the mile of private track skirting the southern boundary of the municipal Bellahouston Park, later host to the 1938 Empire Exhibition. Replaced in June 1960, this was the last South Side route to cross Jamaica Bridge. In 1959 the passengers alighting from 'Cunarder' No 1328 all seem to have briefcases or possibly sports bags. Known officially as 'Mk II Coronations', 100 of these trams, riding on Maley & Taunton bogies and powered by four 36hp motors, were built at Coplawhill between 1948 and 1952. Nowadays the reservation here is grassed over, and in recent times some properties on the Boulevard have suffered from subsidence caused by long-forgotten coal-mine workings. *Vernon Wood*

To the east of Bellahouston Park, at the junction of Cathcart Road and Crown Street, is Caledonia Road United Presbyterian Church (1857), designed by Alexander 'Greek' Thomson. Closed in 1962, it was severely damaged by fire three years later, and from 1966 much of the surrounding housing was also demolished. Although nowadays little more than a shell and isolated in the middle of a gyratory traffic flow, this significant Grade 'A' listed building is destined to become a centre for study and promotion of its designer. Trams had been cleared from this area in 1953, and trolleybuses had last operated on Crown Street (right) in 1966. Between 1949 and 1958 the trolleybuses had replaced a number of tram services, but the transfer of Pinkston Power Station, mounting losses, falling revenue and staff shortages all contributed to their early demise, and this view of TB73 was recorded on 26 May 1967, the penultimate day of trolleybus operation. Note, in front of the church, the public weighbridge, one of a number scattered around the city. *Mike Russell*

Just over a mile to the south of Caledonia Road was a short stretch of paved tramway reservation along Battlefield Road. Photographed from the grounds of today's Langside College, 'Coronation' No 1256 is seen outbound to Holmlea Road on service 5 in June 1957. Off-camera to the left was Langside depot (by then being converted for use by Corporation buses), while towering in the background (right) are the buildings of the Victoria Infirmary (due to be replaced in 2013 by the new South Glasgow Hospital). When opened in 1890 this employed a ground-breaking heating and ventilation system, one of those involved being a young Charles Rennie Mackintosh, the famous Glaswegian architect, who later incorporated this engineering concept in several of his own buildings. Among the low-level structures visible in the centre of the picture is 'The Tonic', a tiny neighbourhood cinema. In 1957, before television became widespread, Glaswegians still supported some 35 central and suburban cinemas, most of which showed double features, with mid-week changes. *Marcus Eavis / Online Transport Archive*

Although trolleybuses first operated from Larkfield bus garage and were later allocated to Govan and Dennistoun tram depots, their main base from 1950 was the purpose-built Hampden garage. Whilst crews were afforded decent facilities, vehicles were provided with rudimentary open storage. To minimise the need for expensive overhead wiring a large sloping concourse allowed for gravity parking and manœuvring. This scene was recorded on the final day, 27 May 1967. Following closure of the trolleybus system the garage was used by other Corporation departments but no longer exists. Evidence of the other Hampden — Scotland's premier international football ground — is apparent to the rear in the form of the floodlighting gantries and mounding for the (then) open terraces. Just three Glasgow trolleybuses survive in preservation.

Mike Russell

In contrast with Hampden garage, Newlands, the largest of the 11 postwar tram depots, was well built, with accommodation for 200 cars. Often allocated newly built trams, it also had its fair share of the traditional 'Standards'. Following the introduction of service numbers, cars wearing Glasgow's famous identifying colours would disappear completely from the city streets by 1952, and on 18 June 1949 the photographer obtained permission to have various cars posed on the depot forecourt, including 'red' 'Standard' No 83. The five colours (blue, green, red, yellow, white) were cleverly arranged so that, other than in a few central locations, no two services with the same colour used the same thoroughfares. Closed to trams in 1960 and to buses in 1986, Newlands depot was subsequently demolished, the forecourt now forming part of a car park for a Morrison's superstore, the main doorways of which, in a nod to the past, depict various trams. *M. H. Waller*

One South Side area to have changed radically since tram days is Old Pollokshaws. Until 1959 trams used a depot-working link between Pollokshaws Road and Kilmarnock Road. Having turned from Pollokshaws Road into Greenview Street, 'Standard' No 234 would continue, partly on single track, by way of Pleasance Street and Coustonholm Road, passing the former Pollokshaws depot, which, despite being replaced by Newlands in 1910, remained extant. The 135 mile tram system had very few single-track sections, and this one was not even protected by signals.

In 1952 a 'Standard' and a 'Cunarder' had collided head-on in broad daylight on a blind corner near the old depot. In this view, unusually, No 234 displays neither a service number nor destination, suggesting that it was out of service. Since the photograph was taken nearly all the property visible in the distance has succumbed to redevelopment, and today there is no direct connection at this point between Pollokshaws Road and Kilmarnock Road. *E. C. Bennett and Martin Jenkins / Online Transport Archive*

This view of a 'Cunarder' passing a field of cows on 6 July 1956 dispels the idea that Glasgow's trams ran only on streets lined with blackened tenements. Operating service 14, No 1299 was on part of the light railway between Barrhead and Spiersbridge, built in 1910 by Paisley District Tramways and purchased by Glasgow in 1923. The fields to the left would later be occupied by the South Nitshill Corporation housing scheme (much of which has since been demolished to make way for owner-occupied semi-detached houses), while the white tower in the distance is Darnley Fire Station.

By the time of this photograph the track was distinctly neglected and when worked by an elderly 'Standard' gave something of a 'white-knuckle' ride. The tram stops' flags announce that 'CARS STOP HERE IF REQUIRED', but there can surely have been few takers, and indeed the 4-mile section between Arden and Crossstobs was abandoned without replacement in September 1956. In 1959 the Arden–Spiersbridge section, the last remnant of the Paisley system, was replaced by part of Corporation bus service 57. *D. G. Clarke*

Left: The first of three rare colour views capturing the rural charm of the outer end of service 14. On 6 July 1956 No 1336, flanked by warning signs, was captured about to cross Nitshill Road into Parkhouse Road, having just covered a short length of reservation away from the road which crossed a tram-only stone bridge (still there today) and a single-track mineral railway leading to a lime and fireclay works. *D. G Clarke*

Below left: In 1941 this location was the scene of a tragic accident when No 976, *en route* to Spiersbridge, lost control down Parkhouse Road and lurched at speed into the sharp bend seen here. Striking a traction pole, it toppled over, three passengers being killed and 22 injured. Staff from the nearby Darnley Fever Hospital provided immediate assistance. Although the accident occurred at night, it was not recorded whether blackout restrictions had been a contributory factor. In this October 1956 view the white-painted pole behind 'Standard' No 256 signifies a section gap in the power-feeder network. *J. G. Todd / Online Transport Archive*

Below: Although Parkhouse Road remains recognisable today, it is difficult to imagine that double track once filled the carriageway, with trams brushing the verges. Here 'Cunarder' No 1309 rolls gently towards Barrhead on the evening of 6 July 1956.
D. G. Clarke

Left: The ancient town of Paisley, Scotland's largest burgh, lies seven miles south-west of Glasgow. Overlooked by the Town Hall (1882), Paisley Cross was the centre of the 18¼-mile Paisley District Tramways network, acquired by Glasgow in 1923, although Glasgow cars first reached the Cross in 1905. Local service 28 (Glenfield–Renfrew Ferry) used the tracks crossing at right-angles, while the curves seen here in the foreground joined the 'main line' westwards to Elderslie and the depot. Even after the takeover the Paisley system resembled an independent small-town operation, with its own depot and workshop. This first of two scenes from 1956 features car No 1003, one of five experimental two-axle trams built between 1939 and 1943. If the war had not intervened, similar 'economy' cars would have followed using equipment purchased to modernise older 'Standard' cars. Relegated mostly to peak-hour duties, these unloved 'Lightweights' ended their days in Govan in 1958. *D. G. Clarke*

Below left: The second scene focuses on the teeming crowds swarming around the central loading islands as 'Cunarder' No 1339 prepares to depart for Elderslie. Behind is the bridge over the River Cart, while to the right is a Leyland PD2 bus belonging to independent operator Smith's of Barrhead — a subsidiary of the Scottish Co-op. The overhead wiring in front of No 1339's bow-collector incorporates a trip device to activate the traffic lights in favour of the tram. *P. J. Marshall*

Paisley was renowned for its weaving and also for its many independent bus operators, one of which, Cunningham's Bus service, seemed to buy better second-hand vehicles than, for example, did Paton Bros of Renfrew. Until in May 1957, when trams on service 28 were replaced by buses from the Scottish Bus Group, Cunningham's and Paton's were among several independents in direct competition along the lucrative 3½-mile Paisley–Renfrew Ferry corridor. Nicknamed 'The Goldmine', the profitable service 28 carried heavy traffic into the commercial centre of Paisley, whilst the rival independents terminated some distance away at St James Street — a tidy walk from the Cross during inclement weather. Seen still with its London Transport bonnet number, Cunningham 18 (ex RT1481) was a Cravens-bodied AEC Regent III dating from 1949 and acquired in 1961. As mass employment declined and car ownership increased, some independents struggled to survive; Cunningham's sold out to Western SMT in 1979. *G. W. Morant*

Left: Renfrew Airport, opened in 1912, was known originally as 'Moorpark Aerodrome', and by the 1930s trams displayed 'Renfrew Aerodrome' on their indicators, calling to mind Fred and Ginger or 1930s Busby Berkeley musicals. When the photographer took this picture on 23 June 1957 he recorded seeing BEA Viscounts and Dakotas and Aer Lingus Dakotas. At that time it was possible to fly to and from London for £7 by using the late-night flight. A coach link from St Enoch Square was provided by Lowland Motorways, using a Strachans-bodied Albion Cheetah (No 29) in a special livery with 'Lowland Greyhound' branding and seen here outside the futuristic terminal building, which resembled today's Clyde Arc Bridge at Finnieston. In 1966 traffic was transferred to the current Glasgow Airport at Abbotsinch, and the site is now occupied by private housing. *Marcus Eavis / Online Transport Archive*

Below left: In April 1960 the legendary Bluebell Girls paid their first-ever visit to the UK, appearing at the Alhambra Theatre. Their arrival, by BEA Viscount, was covered by the press and by one of your authors, although the quality of his camera lens was insufficient to reveal the girls' goose-pimples as they manhandled a giant Easter egg. *Ian Stewart*

In 1951 the so-called Inglis Report recommended that tram services beyond the city boundary should be withdrawn to pave the way for electrification of suburban railways. However, whereas rose bushes benefit from pruning, the same cannot be said of tram services, for the secateurs taken to the outlying branches of the Glasgow network created several artificial termini some distance from logical destinations and, indeed, some in the middle of nowhere, as in the case of 'Hillington Road'. The out-of-boundary services provided hitherto by trams were mostly taken over by the nationalised bus companies, but in the Paisley area there was something of a free-for-all, particularly on the Paisley–Renfrew corridor, where independent operators, along with Western SMT, competed for passengers. Here is Renfrew Cross in happier times, on 7 July 1956, as the crew of 'Standard' No 267, having come all the way from Springburn on a one-time 'blue' service, take their break at the loading island.
D. G. Clarke

The southern slipway of the busy Renfrew chain ferry, a magnet for independent bus operators, was also the northern terminus of tram service 28, from which packed cars departed every few minutes during peak hours. Female crews were first employed during World War 1, and this practice continued until the end. Here the crew of freshly painted 'Standard' No 909 pose for the photographer on 27 May 1956. This car was one of 80 built not at Coplawhill but by the Gloucester Carriage & Wagon Co, in 1900/1; they were not liked by the men at the Car Works (because they had not built them?), but a goodly number had long lives, No 909 surviving until 1958. Postponed because of the Suez oil crisis, withdrawal of the Paisley-area services finally took effect in May 1957. *Vernon Wood*

To facilitate construction of King George V Dock (opened 1931) a lengthy diversion of Renfrew Road was built in 1926 on low-lying land, which led to subsidence, and in 1954 the road and track were raised. In 1958, when the photograph was taken, this roundabout at Shieldhall was on the fringe of the industrial South Side, and scores of peak-hour extras were needed to cater for the substantial workforce employed in the docks, shipyards and associated industries; indeed, when, a few months later, the new trolleybus wiring circling the roundabout was activated it was used *only* by peak-hour journeys on services 106 and 108. 'Standard' No 265 is pictured working service 4 from Springburn, which, following abandonment of the Paisley routes, terminated a short distance ahead at the aforementioned Hillington Road until discontinued in 1958. The buildings in the background, part of the manufacturing arm of the Scottish Co-op, have long since vanished, and the M8 motorway has now diverted much of the traffic away from this location. *Iain Hill / STTS collection*

Once an independent burgh, Govan was incorporated into Glasgow in 1912. The centre of this predominantly working-class community was Govan Cross. Served by trams, buses, trolleybuses, the Subway and nearby cross-river ferries, it was close to shipbuilders Alexander Stephens, Fairfield and Harland & Wolff, as well as Prince's Dock, from where everything from steam locomotives to hairpins went for export. Goods trains, hauled by a little electric locomotive, also used this section of Govan Road. On 2 June 1962,

flags are flying for the Govan Fair. Back then it would have been inconceivable that so much would disappear so quickly, yet even the 9½-mile trolleybus service 106 (Bellahouston–Riddrie/Millerston), introduced in 1958, would last only until 1966. Already many of the once-familiar cast-iron drinking fountains from local foundries have gone, but this one has been painted gold, possibly as part of an early restoration project. Today Govan Cross is little more than a backwater, through traffic having been diverted. *Cedric Greenwood*

Right: The Fairfield Shipbuilding & Engineering Co survives today as BVT, employing state-of-the-art construction techniques. This view, recorded on 2 June 1962, shows vessels assembled on stocks, open to the weather. Prior to painting, the metalwork was shot-blasted before applying red lead, while salt-water corrosion was controlled by attaching sacrificial anodes. *Cedric Greenwood*

Below right: From 1873 Fairfield's transported materials from Govan goods yard along 500yd of street track built to 4ft 7¾in gauge, enabling trams to run on their tyres and railway wagons on their flanges, and in 1905 the operation was electrified. Fairfield's paid Glasgow Corporation for use of the tracks and power, a typical train comprising two to three wagons loaded with steel plates and sections, forgings and timber. This intriguing transfer continued until 1966, by which time Fairfield's last electric locomotive (built 1940 by English Electric) was equipped with twin poles for use on the special trolleybus-type overhead. This evocative scene was recorded on 29 April 1966. Although still a teenager, the photographer had written a polite letter to Fairfield's, seeking permission for its little locomotive to pose at the entrance to the goods yard so that a trolleybus (TB85) and the Plaza cinema could be included in the same frame. Look what happens when you ask nicely. *Mike Russell*

A short distance south of Govan Cross is the main line from Glasgow Central to Paisley and the Clyde Coast. In bygone times Ibrox was the junction for the branch to Govan goods yard and the Docks Railway to Prince's Dock. The branch closed in 1966 along with other inner-suburban stations, including Ibrox, which was convenient for couple of nearby greyhound tracks as well as for Ibrox Park, home of Glasgow Rangers; today there are calls for the station to be reopened to cater for fans heading for the Broomloan Road end. Pictured storming through the station in April 1962 with the 16.52 from St Enoch to Largs is No 45470, one of the ubiquitous 'Black Five' mixed-traffic 4-6-0s designed for the LMS by William (later Sir William) Stanier and introduced from 1934. Note, on the station building (right), the Terence Cuneo poster depicting one of Glasgow's new 'Blue Trains'. Beeching had this poster on his office wall. The original, perhaps? *J. M. Cramp / Colour-Rail SC1449*

On the east side of the Rangers ground is another Ibrox station (formerly Copland Road), this one on the Subway, which Cliff Hanley (who wrote the words for 'Scotland the Brave') described as 'Glasgow's toy train'; it has also been dubbed 'Glasgow's best-kept secret' and, more recently, the 'Clockwork Orange' (recalling Stanley Kubrick's film), after the line was modernised in 1979 with new orange-painted rolling stock. Historically, the 4ft-gauge 6½-mile circular Subway is the third-oldest in the world, beaten only by London and (narrowly) Budapest. The original cable-hauled carriages of 1896 were electrified in 1935 using tramway equipment. These two photographs taken in May 1955 revive memories of the striking livery of lined-out red and cream, the narrow island platforms (with white marks indicating where the first carriage must stop), the art-deco lights and the illuminated destination displays. The non-visible sides of the carriages were painted in overall dark maroon. A programme to dispense with the lattice gates was never completed, some trailers retaining these to the end. *Ray DeGroote / Online Transport Archive (both)*

We now return north with the first of two views of the heart of Govan's dockland, recorded in 1966. The gentlemen on opposite sides of the street are identically dressed and assuming identical poses as TB37, among the first of the 1957 30ft Crossley-bodied BUTs to enter service, approaches the short-working turning circle at Summertown Road. Off camera to the left were three dry docks (1875-98), the longest of which extended 900ft to accommodate two vessels. Until the docks closed, in 1988, ships could be seen towering above Govan Road. Today the basins still look spectacular with their tiered (and now weed-infested) sides.
Mike Russell

At its eastern end Govan Road skirted three sides of the massive Prince's Dock complex; opened in 1897, this was derelict by 1973, but site was later used for the 1988 Garden Festival and is now occupied by the BBC and Scottish Television. The road sloping away to the right of trolleybus TB81 led to the Dock's canting basin. Dominating the scene is the Italianate façade of Govan Town Hall (1901), one of its designers being the son of Alexander 'Greek' Thomson; since stone-cleaned, this too is now a media centre for independent productions. Note that the traction pole on the right of the picture has the span wire attached to a vertical slide rail, enabling the overhead to be raised to allow abnormal loads — such as locomotives or ship's boilers — to pass underneath.
Mike Russell

Cross-river traffic was always a problem, docks and shipyard activity restricting the building of bridges. Even when the Clyde Tunnel opened, in 1958, congestion on George V Bridge prolonged the life of the Finnieston Vehicular Ferry, which carried passengers and vehicles across to Mavisbank Quay, near Prince's Dock. This was one of three vehicular ferries operated by the Clyde Navigation Trust, the others linking Govan with Partick and Linthouse with Whiteinch. Four vessels (with twin screws at either end) were required, one being in reserve. Seen on 27 September 1965, No 3

Finnieston (1937) was 104ft long, 45ft wide and weighed 379 tons. Depending on the tide, the elevating deck could be raised and lowered by as much as 14ft to connect with the slipways, the mechanism being visible on the side. Alongside is diesel-engined free passenger ferry No 10 (1934), which worked the crossing day and night. The ferry closed in 1969 upon opening of the 10-lane Kingston Bridge, which soon became every bit as congested as the George V Bridge had been. *Alex Kerr*

Right: Less than a mile south-east of Finnieston Ferry is the northern extremity of Shields Road. Owing to some tight curves, service 12 — Mount Florida–Paisley Road Toll (Shieldhall in peak hours) — remained a 'Standard' route until replaced by trolleybuses in 1958. No 697 had started life in 1899 with an open top and exposed platforms. Standing on the unprotected step in this view, recorded shortly before the tram's withdrawal in June 1957, a passenger enjoys the breeze. By this time Shields Road was one of only two places with centre bow-string bracket arms, the other being Jamaica Bridge. Note (left) the steaming tar boiler being used in the repair of worn setts. Once the trams were gone most roads were resurfaced with asphalt. Today everything beyond the tram, including the one-time Kinning Park United Free Church, has gone. *Vernon Wood*

Left: In the Shields Road area was a complicated series of railway junctions. Prior to electrification of the Cathcart Circle former passenger locomotive No 54465, a 4-4-0 built by the Caledonian Railway at its St Rollox Works in 1916, hauls a 'Blue Train' into sidings near Shields Road station in April 1962. In the past, spare stock was held in sidings ready to be used at short notice — and just as well, for following the much-heralded introduction of the 'Blue Trains' in November 1960 teething troubles led to their mass withdrawal on 18 December; amazingly, sufficient locomotives and carriages were found to provide a full steam service the next day. However, these EMUs (later Class 303), designed to a very high standard, ultimately clocked up 42 years of service. *R. Oakley / Colour Rail SC1116*

On the short stretch from Paisley Road Toll to Shields Road trams on service 12 (and subsequently the replacement single-decker trolleybuses) negotiated several right-angle turns. Photographed on an enthusiasts' tour on 25 February 1967, TB109 is seen navigating the second of these into Seaward Street. In the cutting (out of view beyond the fence on the right) was the former Caledonian Railway branch which fed into a massive splay of sidings to the east of Prince's Dock, while in the distance can be seen the industrial bulk of the 'General Terminus Quay', where iron ore was unloaded from ships directly onto goods wagons — an operation deemed sufficiently impressive to feature in one of Terence Cuneo's BR publicity paintings. (The structure has now gone.) During preparations for the 1988 Garden Festival serious consideration was given to bringing the Festival tramway up the cutting (by then abandoned) to connect with the Shields Road Subway station, but this was thwarted by an inability to gain sufficient clearance beneath the bridge carrying traffic along Paisley Road. *Mike Russell*

Left: Served first by horse trams in 1872, Paisley Road Toll developed into a significant transport hub supporting a forest of overhead wires. The last service trams passed through in 1958, leaving trolleybuses to continue for a further nine years. Recorded on 29 April 1966, this view of the junction, overlooked by the 'Angel' building (left, fronted by a long-gone tram shelter), shows Paisley Road West (left) and Govan Road (right) both feeding into Paisley Road, while off-camera to the left is Admiral Street, whence the last trolleybuses would depart in 1967. To the right of TB53, beyond the Mavisbank galvanising works, can be seen the massive Finnieston Crane (now preserved). Two decades later this area would be occupied by the tramway constructed for the 1988 Garden Festival. All buildings in Govan Road, including the warehouse with the onion dome, have now been replaced by low-density housing, while the 'Angel' building is now home to 'Il Fiorentino' — one of Glasgow's best Italian restaurants. *Mike Russell*

Above right: About a mile east of Paisley Road Toll, close to the river, is Clyde Place. Although slow-moving vehicles and hand carts were banned from some city streets no such restrictions applied here, although by 20 September 1967 this magnificent Clydesdale horse, with its huge load of Black & White whisky barrels, was redolent of an earlier bygone era, when the streets were dominated by the sight, sounds and smells of thousands of horses. In the background (left) can be seen the dockside sheds at Bridge Wharf and, beyond, George V Bridge and the railway bridge leading to Central station.

Right: Although Clyde Place is now cut off at West Street and fashionable flats have been built on the small, filled-in Kingston Dock (1867-1966), in 1967 the carter still crossed the water passageway to the dock by the swing bridge; it was then possible to plod along cobbled dockside roads as far as Prince's Dock to emerge into Govan Road. *J. G. Parkinson / Online Transport Archive*

When it opened in 1928 George V Bridge alleviated pressure on Jamaica Bridge by offering an alternative river crossing and was used by several key tram services linking the city to Paisley and Renfrew, all of which were replaced during 1957/8. Heading north towards Springburn on service 27 in June 1957 is No 643, the last of three cars to overturn on the sharp bend at the foot of Bilsland Drive (see page 21), as a result of which it had been rebuilt in 1947. Catching the evening sun, it is pursued by three Corporation buses, of which the newly delivered Daimler CVG6 leading is occupying the crown of the road prior to making a right turn to reach its stance below the bridge leading into Central station. Visible on the left are the various signal gantries marking the approach to the station, while embedded in the setts (right) are large slabs forming a wagonway for horse-drawn traffic, making for a smoother and easier passage; these were known as 'wheelers' or 'cart tramrails', and a few still survive. *Marcus Eavis / Online Transport Archive*

This nostalgic journey ends north of the Clyde in the central area once served by four railway termini, two of which — Buchanan Street and St Enoch — were closed in 1966. The latter, with its magnificent arch, opened in 1876 and was the first public building in Glasgow to be lit by electricity; enlarged in 1904, it remained slightly smaller than Central but had the largest of all the city's the railway hotels. When photographed on 11 April 1959 Class 2P 4-4-0 No 40621 — one of a class of 136 introduced by the LMS in 1928, albeit to an earlier Midland Railway design — was in charge of an empty-stock working. Even towards the end, 250 trains per day operated from the station to destinations such as Dumfries, Ayr, Largs and Stranraer, as well as points on the Midland main line to St Pancras. The station was demolished following closure, and indeed all the industrial buildings seen here have gone, swept away in the construction of the St Enoch Shopping Centre. *Paul de Beer / Online Transport Archive*

Left: Between 1929 and 2001 elegant St Enoch Square had as its focal point a selection of stances for Corporation buses. Still in traditional livery in the early 1960s, D19, a 1949 Daimler CVD6 with Northern Coachbuilders body, departs for Castlemilk on service 14. The timber-framed bodies on these buses soon worked loose but after strengthening at Larkfield garage would last as long as their steel-framed contemporaries, D19 remaining in service until 1965. *Ian Dunnett / Online Transport Archive*

Below left: Used by Central and Western SMT, Waterloo Street bus station (1927-71) consisted originally of a series of platforms with lattice gates to control access to departing buses. As vehicle length and width increased — witness extra-long Central SMT Bristol Lodekka BL285 — the terminus became very cramped, but removal of the gates only encouraged passengers to spill over into the bus 'territory', and drivers faced a very sharp turn into Waterloo Street which was often blocked opposite the exit by indiscriminate parking. Redeveloped twice since closure of the bus station, the site now houses the Clydesdale Bank Exchange building. *Ian Stewart*

Today Glasgow has two rail termini — Queen Street (1842) and Central (1879). In recent years both have benefited from major investment which has effectively eliminated all traces of the steam age. However, the pattern of services at Central has changed little over the intervening years and comprises a mix of expresses and cross-country services along with inner- and outer-suburban workings. This view of Platform 12, recorded on 1 August 1966, during the dying days of steam, revives memories of soot-grimed walls and roofs. Waiting to depart bunker-first for Weymss Bay is No 80045, a BR Standard 2-6-4 tank engine of a design introduced in 1951. Steam would finally be ousted from Central in April 1967, and the diesel multiple-unit standing at Platform 13 (left) symbolises the future. In 2008 these platforms were renumbered in preparation for the abortive Glasgow Airport Rail Link.
Martin Jenkins / Online Transport Archive

It seems appropriate to conclude this bygone journey in Argyle Street, the UK's last great tram thoroughfare. On this major east-west axis trams reigned supreme until 1961, and at peak times an endless procession ran nose-to-tail in both directions, swallowing up huge crowds, the buildings echoing to the sounds of bells, wheels and motors. However, by 2 June 1962, when this photograph was taken, only two services remained. 'Coronation' No 1269, in the foreground, at the junction with Buchanan Street, still has its original art-deco lighting and as such has been selected to work a private tour organised by the (then) Scottish Tramway Museum Society. The intention was to donate this car to the National Tramway Museum, but unfortunately the body proved to be in poor condition, so No 1282 was substituted, taking the lighting and bogies from No 1269. It is fitting that several 'Coronations' survive as potent reminders of the value of electric traction, and one can only hope that Glasgow, like Edinburgh and so many other world-class cities, will one day benefit from a modern, efficient and environmentally friendly light-rail network. *Cedric Greenwood*